THE HEROES
OF 9/11

BY BARBARA FIFER

Editorial Offices: Glenview, Illinois • Parsippany, New Jersey • New York, New York

Sales Offices: Needham, Massachusetts • Duluth, Georgia • Glenview, Illinois
Coppell, Texas • Sacramento, California • Mesa, Arizona

Terrorist Attacks

September 11, 2001, began as a clear autumn morning in the northeastern United States. Then an airplane crashed into one of the World Trade Center's Twin Towers in New York City. At first it seemed to be an accident, but eighteen minutes later another plane crashed into the second tower. Thirty-seven minutes after that, a third passenger plane crashed into the Pentagon in Arlington, Virginia. Passengers on a fourth plane, Flight 93, fought back against the terrorists, and their plane crashed in a field.

Terrorists had **hijacked**, or took over by force, the planes. Those men were angry at the United States. They flew three planes into those buildings on purpose.

Many people became heroes that day. This book is about a few of them.

Thousands of people were working in the World Trade Center in New York City on the morning of September 11, 2001.

Here is a view of the World Trade Center buildings as seen before the attack.

The World Trade Center

Seven buildings made up the World Trade Center. The buildings stood in New York City, on Manhattan Island. Businesses rented space in six of those buildings. The seventh building was a hotel. When the attacks happened, at least forty thousand people were in the buildings.

The two most famous buildings were known by several names. They were called the Twin Towers, North Tower and South Tower, or WTC1 and WTC2. They were 110 stories high—among the world's six tallest buildings. Each tower had ninety-seven elevators for people and six elevators for freight.

This is the Pentagon. It is large enough that the United States Capitol could fit into one of its five sides.

Named for Its Shape

Pentagon is the name for a five-sided figure. The United States Department of Defense has its home in a building built in that shape. It is simply called "the Pentagon." The Pentagon is across the Potomac River from Washington, D.C.

The Pentagon is five stories tall and covers twenty-nine acres. The total length of its halls is seventeen-and-a-half miles.

This is the **headquarters**, or main office, of all the branches of the United States military. About twenty-six thousand employees work in the Pentagon.

Four Airplanes

Around eight o'clock on the morning of September 11, 2001, four airplanes took off with terrorists on board. The terrorists hijacked one plane and crashed it into the World Trade Center's North Tower. Shortly after, the same thing happened with another plane that hit the South Tower.

A third plane left Washington, D.C. Terrorists hijacked the plane and turned it back toward Washington, D.C. They crashed it into the Pentagon.

The fourth plane was Flight 93. A few people on board heard about the first three crashes on their cell phones. When terrorists took over their plane, some of the passengers fought back. The plane, which was also headed for Washington, D.C., crashed in a field in Pennsylvania.

Terrorists crashed an airplane into each of the World Trade Center's Twin Towers.

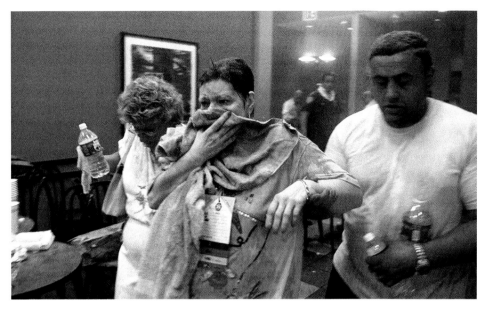

Many Twin Towers workers helped others get down the stairs and outside.

Helping Each Other

Michael Benfante and John Cerqueira worked in the World Trade Center. Their office was on the eighty-first floor of the North Tower. It was four floors below where Flight 11 hit.

Going down the stairs, the men had a hard time breathing and seeing. The airplane's fuel was burning and filling the building with thick, black smoke.

On the sixty-eighth floor, they met a woman in a wheelchair. Using a special rescue chair, the men carried her down the stairs. It took an hour.

In the South Tower, Welles Crowther carried some people part of the way down. He also asked healthy people to help others who were hurt.

Firefighters, Police, and EMTs

Firefighters and medical workers called EMTs, or emergency medical technicians, rushed upstairs as office workers climbed down the stairs in the Twin Towers. Each firefighter carried sixty pounds of gear. Other firefighters fought smaller fires on the ground. EMTs treated injured people outside.

The two airplanes each held twenty-four thousand gallons of jet fuel. The crashes caused hot fires that weakened the towers' steel frames. The North Tower stood for about one hundred minutes, and the South Tower stood for sixty minutes. Thousands of people escaped the towers.

Finally, the towers' steel frames gave way and the buildings fell. The 343 firefighters inside were killed. Twenty-three police officers were also killed. Later, WTC (Building) 7 and the hotel collapsed.

The New York Fire Department crews arrived at the Twin Towers and began rescuing people within minutes.

Fire departments from around the area came to help the Pentagon's own firefighters.

Pentagon Rescuers

The Pentagon has its own police and firefighters, but many nearby firefighters came to help. Soldiers dug tunnels under furniture and fallen walls so people could crawl out. One large man held up a ceiling for a while.

Victor Correa, a lieutenant colonel in the army, walked through smoke in a dark hallway. Over and over, he yelled, "Listen to me! Follow my voice!" He led many people outdoors.

Staff Sergeant Christopher Braman, a Marine, heard a woman clapping. She could not shout, and was badly burned. He rescued her.

Land the Airplanes!

The Federal Aviation Administration (FAA) sets the rules for non-military airplanes. After the first two crashes, the FAA stopped planes from taking off and told air traffic controllers to have all other planes land.

Air traffic controllers talk to pilots during takeoffs and landings. The controllers have to be calm in emergencies. Now they had to land nearly four thousand planes at once! Only military planes were allowed to fly.

No one knew if terrorists were aboard anymore airliners. By about noon, all airliners had landed.

Air traffic controllers watch images of airplanes on computers while they talk with the pilots by radio.

Restaurants, Stores, and Hotels Help

When the Twin Towers collapsed in New York City, the air was filled with smoke and dust. Thousands of people were still walking away.

Restaurants, stores, and hotels opened their doors. People could go in for a drink of water. Usually, this was for customers only.

Subways and trains stopped running. People had to walk home—sometimes long distances. Stores gave free running shoes to people who needed them.

A fancy hotel set up beds and cots in its ballroom. The chef cooked lots of food. Rescue workers were welcome to eat and rest.

That night some people had to sleep on the streets. Hotels lent them pillows and blankets.

When the Twin Towers fell, they sent a thick, dark cloud of smoke and dust through parts of New York City.

Rescue workers searched for trapped survivors at the
Twin Towers all through the night of September 11, 2001.

Digging for Survivors

People were still escaping to other parts of New York.
Rescue workers were already digging for survivors at the Twin
Towers.

In New York and at the Pentagon, police and firefighters
came from near and far. So did doctors, nurses, and EMTs.
Construction workers brought heavy machines.

Owners brought their search-and-rescue dogs. The dogs
crawled into small spaces, walked on broken glass, and sniffed
and listened for survivors.

Spotlights allowed rescuers to work all night. They found a
few survivors.

Thousands of people gave blood to help those injured in the attacks.

People Make Donations

Within four days, more than 250,000 people donated blood. Usually, in four days, only about 91,000 people do that. Injured people often need new blood to help them heal.

In New York City, Robin Merendino and her family went to restaurants and supermarkets to ask for free hot food for rescuers. Soon they had 1,500 pounds of meals that filled five vans!

Gifts from Everywhere

The New York Fire Department lost ninety-one fire trucks, rescue trucks, and cars when the Twin Towers fell. People from Louisiana, Ohio, and Utah bought new fire trucks for the department. Schoolchildren in Columbia, South Carolina, held a fundraiser and bought New York City a new fire truck. Two companies that build fire trucks each donated a truck.

Schools, clubs, and businesses across the United States raised money for those harmed by the attacks. Some money was used for educating children who lost relatives. Some money helped people who had to move out of damaged apartments. Some money was used for medical care.

Individual citizens, companies, and other groups donated many kinds of things to survivors and rescuers.

The last piece of steel was removed from the World Trade Center wreckage eight months after the attacks.

Sympathy and Changes

Nations around the world expressed sympathy for the United States' losses. "Today we are all Americans," said a former prime minister of Israel. He meant that everyone shared in the sadness.

People worked day and night to clean up the World Trade Center site. Trucks carried away broken steel and cement. They finished on May 30, 2002—three months earlier than expected. A contest was held to choose a design for new buildings to replace the ones destroyed.

Airports made many changes in how they checked passengers onto airliners. They wanted to make it impossible for terrorists to take over airplanes ever again.

New Buildings and Memorials

More than 3,000 people died in the four attacks on September 11, 2001. More than 2,500 people survived with injuries. These people were from many states, the District of Columbia, as well as other nations.

New buildings will be built where the Twin Towers stood in New York City along with a **memorial**, a way to remember and honor a person or an event. The damaged part of the Pentagon was repaired in eleven months. The National Park Service plans to build a memorial where Flight 93 crashed in Pennsylvania. Everyone who helped during and after the attacks is a hero of 9/11.

A single 1,776-foot tower will replace the Twin Towers.

Glossary

headquarters the center of operations for a company or a military unit

hijack to take control of a moving vehicle by use of force

memorial a building, statue, park, or other creation that honors certain people or events

pentagon a shape with five equal sides

terrorist a person who uses violence and fear to try to achieve goals